MINISTERIAL ETHICS

ETHICS

Second Edition

DAG HEWARD-MILLS

Parchment House

MINISTERIAL ETHICS

Copyright © 1999 Dag Heward-Mills

Originally published 1998 by Parchment House
ISBN: 978-9988-7798-1-X
6th Printing 2007

Second edition published 2014 by Parchment House
16th Printing 2018

[77]Find out more about Dag Heward-Mills at:
Healing Jesus Campaign
Write to: evangelist@daghewardmills.org
Website: www.daghewardmills.org
Facebook: Dag Heward-Mills
Twitter: @EvangelistDag

ISBN : 978-1-61395-487-4

Dedication:
To *Moses Kweku Baiden Snr.*, my father-in-law
Thank you for the many valuable things I have learnt through you.
You have been a second father to me.

Contents

1. Why Ethics?...1

2. Ethics for the Head...4

3. Ethics for Assistants...11

4. Ethics for Resignations and Departures.........................20

5. Ethics for the Church Service.....................................25

6. Ethics for Interacting with Church Members..............28

7. Ethics for Relating with the Opposite Sex...................33

8. Ethics for Relating with External Ministers................36

9. Ethics for Handling Visiting Ministers.......................43

10. Ethics for the Travelling Minister..............................47

11. Financial Ethics...52

12. Ethics for Receiving of Gifts.....................................57

13. The Ethics of Privacy..59

14. Ethics for Public Appearance....................................62

15. Ethics for Handling Outsiders...................................65

CHAPTER 1

Why Ethics?

...that thou mayest know how thou oughtest to
BEHAVE THYSELF in the house of God...
1 Timothy 3:15

Ministers are under a lot of pressure. The pressures of finances, the pressures of family and the pressures of human expectations are just a few of the many demands of ministry. These pressures in the Lord's work are often the causes of improper behaviour of pastors.

In the ministry, improper conduct can create an unfortunate misrepresentation of what we stand for in the ministry. At no time in the history of Christianity has the conduct and lifestyle of the clergy come under such scrutiny. We, who are called into this ministry have to fight to maintain certain standards. The world is watching us, hoping to find something wrong so that they can persecute us. That is why Paul said that ministers should have a good report even with unbelievers.

Moreover he must have a good report of them which are without; lest he fall into reproach and the snare of the devil.

1 Timothy 3:7

When God calls a man, He calls him first to follow Him, and then to learn of Him. We are never to stop learning. The ministry is a long road of continuous education. One of the things that Paul instructed us to learn of him was his manner of life. In other words, we are to follow the ethical principles that influenced his behaviour as a minister.

But thou hath fully known my doctrine, MANNER OF LIFE...

2 Timothy 3:10

So what are ministerial ethics? These are the standards, principles and broad guidelines we must observe in the ministry. Ethical practices are upright, sound, honourable, moral, lawful, above-board, and full of integrity.

Unethical behaviour on the other hand, is that which is indecent, unfair, improper, dishonourable, shady, unscrupulous and maybe even crooked.

What Ethics Are Not

Ethical guidelines are not absolute laws. They are not the law of God. Ethics are not scriptures and you will find that some of them even became impractical at different seasons of the ministry. However, they are generally helpful guidelines for practicing ministry. Not living according some of these ethics is not necessarily a sin. They are just ideas that may help us to fulfil our ministries. I am presenting these biblical guidelines to help ministers live and minister with wisdom.

It is my prayer that you will find within these pages, something that is profitable for instruction in righteousness, that you - the man of God – "...may be perfect, thoroughly furnished unto all good works" (2 Timothy 3:17).

CHAPTER 2

Ethics for the Head

There is an evil which I have seen under the sun, as an error which proceedeth from the ruler:

Ecclesiastes 10:5

I n any church, only one person can be the head or senior minister. Good things can come out of the head, but errors can also proceed from that level.

The head is the visionary of the church. In order to bear much fruit, the head must accept that he cannot work alone. He has to work with a team of people. It is the existence of this team that makes him the head.

The art of being a head is the art of leading a team. To develop an effective team and efficiently run it, the head must establish a close-working relationship with associates and junior ministers. Share the burden of the ministry with others and you will be a greater and more productive person.

Being a successful Head involves trusting people enough to share the great responsibility that is on you. Heads of churches do many unethical things in their capacity as leaders of the team. These unethical actions lead to the disintegration of the teams and churches.

A team that breaks up every few years is never going to grow very large. The break up of pastoral teams is one of the problems of modern ministry. Perhaps, forty per cent of the causes of rebellion can be attributed to the heads, forty per cent to the assistants, and twenty per cent to a combination of the heads and the assistants.

The team consists of the different people you work with. They may be associate pastors, choir directors, worship leaders, editors, administrators, and so on.

I will now outline a few ethical practices that senior ministers will do well to follow:

1. Let everyone know that you are the head, and that you "know" that you are the head.

People tend to take advantage of weak leaders. Wives take advantage of weak husbands. Your assistants will dominate you and capitalize on your lack of decisiveness and confidence. Take charge! Apostle Paul introduced himself very confidently and always emphasized who he was.

Paul, an apostle, (not of men, neither by man, but by Jesus Christ...)

Galatians 1:1

2. **Let your associates be aware that in as much as they are important to you, they are not indispensable.**

   Your assistants must know that you are not afraid of them. They are privileged to stand by your side, and must keep their rank or else... Your associate should not feel that he is the one holding the ministry together. Your assistants must know that they can be dismissed. Any person you cannot control, instruct or direct should not be your associate. He probably sees himself as more of an equal, but there can be only one head. Anything with two heads is a freak. There can only be one head - and this must be clear to everyone.

3. **Let all your associates and assistants know and understand what you are trying to achieve.**

   If you are trying to build a large church, let them understand what it means to do so. If you are trying to win souls, let them understand the cost of evangelism.

   If three or four people try to move a huge object without clearly knowing exactly where they are moving it to, you only have an awkward and frustrated team. I often tell my people, "Listen, I want to finish this project by the end of the month." This helps them to adjust to the extra stresses and pressures that will arise.

4. **Tell everyone in the team what exactly is expected of them.**

   An undefined role leads to confusion and a feeling of worthlessness. This is not good for the morale of the team.

5. **Each person must know his or her rank.**

   The head is not respected when the order of ranking is unclear. People assume that everyone is equal, but that is a big mistake. Everyone cannot be the same.

6. **Let every member of the ministry team know what the other members of the team are supposed to do.**

   This helps each member to know what to expect from the others.

7. **Each team member must have a section over which he has complete responsibility.**

   Every team member has many duties. There must be a specific area for which everyone is accountable. Responsibility for an entire section provides the team member with a sense of importance.

8. **Give praise and recognition to your assistants and team members in public.**

   If you want your assistant to repeat a good thing he has done, remember to praise him specifically for that accomplishment. I guarantee you that he will repeat it. Public praise increases confidence, and motivates your associates to work harder. Public praise also stimulates a spirit of loyalty.

9. **Rebuke and correct your assistants in private.**

   It is difficult to lead people after you have been corrected like a little child before them. Though some of the leaders are still in training, the church needs to have confidence in them.

   Public criticism can be degrading, and will often generate thoughts about resignation. Criticism should be constructive, and not destructive. Remember that you are trying to build up associates and not tear them down.

10. Accept 100% responsibility for anything that goes wrong.

Remember that Adam was blamed ultimately for the fall of mankind though it was the woman who directly brought about the fall. The fact is that as the Head, you are responsible for everything that goes on. If you want the privileges, you must also accept the blame!

11. Do not complain about your associates.

To complain about or to condemn a ministry team member is actually to blame yourself. Why did you accept them to work with you in the first place? Complaining provides a breeding ground for disunity and disloyalty. When the Head complains, he demonstrates to all others that complaining is all right.

12. Do not suppress your assistants. Give advice on how to do it better.

Be a teacher of your subordinates. See yourself as the coach of a team. Guide them into becoming better people. Do not try to keep people down. Because you cannot really keep a good man down. Be a "way-maker" for the up-and-coming minister.

13. Regard your associates as the most important people in the church.

They are the people who will either make or break you.

14. Treat your assistants and associates as friends.

Henceforth I call you not servants... but I have called you friends...

John 15:15

The senior minister must develop close relationships with those in his ministry team. Such close relationships will produce a stronger and more loyal team. Working closely with assistants in the ministry brings about valuable friendships that could last a lifetime.

It is extremely important that you, as the senior minister (even if you are reserved or quiet by nature) make a conscious effort to build these important friendships.

How to Build Friendships in the Ministry

1. **Build friendships by accepting one another.**

   Jesus accepted a variety of people from different backgrounds to be His friends and co-workers. The ministry brings people together from all walks of life. You may not, naturally speaking, have become friends but the work of the ministry can make you into close friends. Appreciate the good qualities in your other team members. Show them praise and admiration as often as possible.

   ...he saw Levi...sitting at the receipt of custom, and said unto him, Follow me...

   Mark 2:14

2. **Build friendships by eating together.**

   Jesus ate regularly with His disciples. He therefore developed very close relationships with His disciples.

   And as they were eating, Jesus took bread...and gave it to the disciples...

   Matthew 26:26

3. **Build friendships by moving around together.**

   Jesus went from place to place with His disciples. Jesus even went to His hometown with Hs ministry colleagues!

   And he went out from thence, and came into his own country; and his disciples follow him.

   Mark 6:1

4. **Build friendships by praying and ministering together.**

   Jesus took His disciples for prayer meetings in gardens.

...he went forth with his disciples over the brook...
where was a garden, into the which he entered, and his
disciples.

John 18:1

5. **Build friendships by travelling together.**

Jesus travelled with His friends.

**And when they (Jesus and the disciples) came nigh to
Jerusalem...**

Mark 11:1

6. **Build friendships by waiting on the Lord together.**

Jesus did that!

**And after six days Jesus taketh with him Peter, and
James, and John, and leadeth them up unto an high
mountain apart by themselves...**

Mark 9:2

CHAPTER 3

Ethics for Assistants

And if ye have not been faithful in that which is
another man's, who shall give you that which is your
own?

Luke 16:12

The assisting minister is anyone operating as an associate pastor, assistant pastor, worship leader, departmental pastor, youth pastor, branch pastor, minister of music, etc.

The obligations of an assisting minister may look obvious. It may even seem superfluous to write about what is expected of the assisting minister. However, I have found the assisting minister to be one of the most important people in the ministry team. He can make or break the ministry by his actions, words and even attitude. It is better to have no assistant, than to have a bad assistant. It is better to have no branch church than to have a bad branch pastor.

A good assistant minister is compared to a good ambassador. He does not reflect his own ideas and visions --only those of his home country (senior minister). A good assistant minister can be compared to a good wife. He must obey instructions and *genuinely support* the head. He must not be an independent or "difficult to control" person. If you are not faithful with another man's ministry, do not ever expect to have your own.

There is a proliferation of Absaloms, Adonijahs, Ahithophels, Shemeis, Joabs, Judases and Lucifers in the church. These are the major rebels of the Bible. Every minister will have his fair share of these personalities. I am against these people, and I constantly teach about them in order to expose them. Decide that you will never become a rebel! In your position as an assistant minister, you will have to observe certain rules of conduct.

The following guidelines will help you to be a good assistant:

1. Make mention of your Head and senior often.

Whenever you are speaking, preaching or counselling, make favorable references to him. As I said earlier, you are actually an ambassador representing him.

2. Genuinely admire your Head and praise him often.

If you do not admire your leader, you should not be working with him in the first place!

3. **Introduce your Head in an exciting way and make positive or complimentary remarks about everything that he has preached.**

   Make statements like, "I was really blessed today by this message", or "That message was timely."

4. **Do not become a receiver of complaints.**

   If your office is a centre for the discussion of the shortcomings of your pastor, surely, you are another Absalom in the making!

   And Absalom rose up early, and stood beside the way... and it was so, that when any man that had a controversy came... then Absalom called unto him... And Absalom said unto him, See, thy matters are good... but there is no man deputed of the king... Oh that I were made judge...

   2 Samuel 15:2-4

5. **You must find genuine excuses for any lapses in the Head.**

   Everybody makes mistakes, and nobody is always right. Your senior will have his fair share of mistakes. It is your duty as a good assistant to defend and protect the developing ministry of your pastor.

6. **Whenever your Head is unable to attend a function, you must inform the parties concerned that your Head had intended to be there himself but could not make it for very good reasons.**

   You must give the impression that your Head is a good person who is constrained by real and pressing schedules. Do not say, "Oh, I do not know why he didn't come to the hospital to visit you. He is probably sleeping at home!"

7. **Always remind the congregation that you are not the main person, and that there is someone above you.**

   When people are very impressed with your ministry, tell them happily that there is someone greater than you. Notice what John the Baptist did when he was in a similar situation. He said,

...I am NOT the Christ, but...I am sent...

John 3:28

8. **Show your admiring congregation how and where you learnt all that you know.**

   Jesus often said,

   ...The Son can do nothing of himself, but what he seeth the Father do...

   John 5:19

9. **When you minister to church members let them know that you are actually doing it on behalf of the Head.**

   When we say, "In the name of Jesus" it informs people that we are acting on behalf of Jesus, our Head.

10. **Be genuinely happy at the promotion of your Head.**

   Do not secretly think that he does not deserve the fame that he is getting. Notice what John the Baptist said when he heard that Jesus was becoming very popular:

   And they came unto John, and said unto him, Rabbi, he that was with thee beyond Jordan, to whom thou barest witness, behold, the same baptizeth, AND ALL MEN COME TO HIM.

   John 3:26

   Notice again the classic reply of a good assistant:

   He must increase, but I must decrease.

   John 3:30

11. **Ensure that everything is well with your Head.**

   Ensure that he has a seat and is comfortable. Give up your own chair if necessary. Ensure that he is acknowledged and respected by all. This is the duty of a good assistant.

Be genuinely excited at the arrival and involvement of your Head Pastor in any function.

You must announce the visit of your senior to your department or branch with excitement. If you see his involvement as an intrusion and a bother, then you have a problem. You are probably a rebellious assistant at heart!

12. Honour your Head's wife as well. Minister to her and give her gifts.

I take note of any person who doesn't respect my wife. It is an important sign to me.

He that receiveth you receiveth me...
Matthew 10:40

If you receive my wife, you have received me. In the same way, if you disrespect and disregard my wife, you have done the same to me.

13. Regard your association with your pastor as a learning experience.

Decide to learn something from him everyday.

14. Acquire your pastor's tapes and books.

"Soak in" his messages on audio and video tapes. Catch the anointing on his life through faithfulness and loyalty. As a good assistant, you must take notes, say "Amen" and smile when your Head is speaking, teaching or even counselling. The congregation will follow whatever the assistant does.

15. In your preaching, do not hesitate to refer to your Head as an example of a successful person. Use him as an illustration for noble things.

16. Do not *publicly* disagree with policies and decisions made by the Head.

17. It is unethical for an assistant to establish a private, side-fellowship in the church without the knowledge or approval of the Head.

18. Periodically organize pleasant surprises for your Head.

Spontaneously celebrate the birthday of your Head, and give gifts to him. This will draw you closer to his heart.

A man's gift maketh room for him, and bringeth him before great men.

Proverbs 18:16

19. When your Head is travelling, you must be at the airport to see him off.

Be there to welcome him with joy when he returns. On some occasions you must organize a 'welcome home' party. Let him know that you are glad to have him back!

20. During counselling sessions you must assist properly.

Do not contribute any counsel that is contrary to what is being said. Do not try to develop a completely new train of thought. This may only be confusing to the one receiving counsel. Do not try to impress anyone with some "high sounding" wisdom. Simply help your senior to say what he is saying better and emphasize what he has already said. Do not remain quiet during counselling sessions. This will make you look like a spectator and will make the person being counselled feel uncomfortable.

21. I teach all assisting ministers to use these simple but very powerful phrases whilst assisting their seniors in counselling:

1. Do you understand what Pastor is saying?

2. Do you understand that Pastor is only trying to help you?

3. Pastor is only saying this because he loves you.

4. I wish I had had someone speak to me this way when I was in a similar situation.

As you interject comments like these during counselling sessions, you lend a greater impact to his words.

A bad assistant is often difficult to detect. The Bible teaches us to mark them that cause divisions. Senior ministers must be able to identify unethical behaviour in assisting ministers. Assisting ministers should identify any of these traits and judge themselves.

22. Do not be happy when your head makes a mistake.

A bad assistant is one who, when things go wrong, is quick to say, "I knew all along that this would not work."

23. Do not be a silent assistant.

When you come up with a suggestion, new idea or vision, a bad assistant has no comment to make - either good or bad. Silence is often indicative of someone who is not in full agreement. Silent people are often thinking, "I would be a better Head if I had the chance!"

24. Don't be a position-conscious assistant. A position-conscious assistant will stretch out his hand to take the Head's place. He will try to use his pastor's absence to establish himself as someone who is "just as good".

25. Do not look out for faults in your head.

Bad assistants are people who see faults in most of their pastor's actions.

26. Do not present yourself as 'more approachable' than your head pastor.

Some members of the flock seem to find their way to these bad assistants with complaints.

Often they say, "He is more approachable than the Head Pastor." Watch out for these so-called "approachable" assistants.

27. Say a hearty 'Amen' when your head is speaking.

They do not clap, smile, say "Amen", shout, or laugh when the Head is preaching. These bad assistants look like diplomatic know-it-alls.

28. Flow with the mood of the congregation.

If the congregation is happy, make sure that you are happy too. Do not present yourself as someone who is not easily impressionable or gullible. They do not flow with the general mood of the congregation.

When everybody is laughing, the bad assistant does not laugh. On a good day, he may afford a faint smile. When everybody is exclaiming in agreement, he may give a diplomatic nod of consent. When everybody's hands are raised, he lifts up only one hand. You see, these bad assistants are simply not as impressed as the rest of the church.

29. Be happy when your head is promoted.

Bad assistants are not happy at the blessings of their senior pastor.

They feel he has too much anyway. They feel that they do the "donkey work" while he gets all the rewards. He thinks in his heart, "Monkey dey work, baboon dey chop", as they say in Africa.

Instead of seeing certain things as necessary privileges accompanying the office of a Head, they are constantly unhappy (whether openly or secretly) about any honour or privilege bestowed on the Head. They consider all these as frivolous and a waste of resources. You will notice that the one who thought like this during the times of Jesus was the betrayer, Judas.

Then took Mary a pound of ointment... very costly, and anointed the feet of Jesus... Then saith one of his disciples, Judas...Why was not this ointment... given to the poor?

John 12:3-5

30. Do not allow thoughts of resignation to be in you.

Bad assistants constantly have thoughts flashing through their minds about leaving the church. They may come to you and say they are confused as to whether they are in the will of God or not. They are always unsure about whether they should be with you.

31. Make extra efforts to help with the vision.

Be careful of assistants who make no extra efforts. Notice people who do not make any "extra" efforts outside their specified duties.

It is only ethical for a pastor to strive to achieve greater things for the Lord. He should on his own accord work for extra hours. It should not be necessary to have to drive an assisting pastor. A lazy and reluctant assistant may be a dangerous assistant to have around.

32. Notice people who have "empty" and non-spiritual wives. They can turn out to be bad assistants.

Empty wives are prone to stirring up discontent in the assistant pastor's mind. They pass comments and suggest things that make the Assistant Pastor feel dissatisfied with his position. These "empty" wives think mainly of physical comfort, public impressions and their status in the church. They are often unaware of the spiritual implications of the advice they give. Some wives make their husbands do unethical things.

But Jezebel his wife came to him, and said unto him,WHY IS THY SPIRIT SO SAD... Dost thou now govern the kingdom of Israel? arise, and eat bread, and let thine heart be merry: I WILL GIVE THEE THE VINEYARD OF NABOTH THE JEZREELITE.

1 Kings 21:5, 7

CHAPTER 4

Ethics for Resignations and Departures

Leaving a church or ministry (resignation, in other words) is something that happens - whether we like it or not. At times, people who never intended to leave a ministry are forced to resign.

Resignation is rarely happens in a cordial atmosphere. Resignation in the church setting usually occurs in the midst of misunderstandings, conflicts, accusations, unhealed wounds and ingratitude. I have rarely seen a peaceful departure. Departures and resignations may be biblically necessary because

i.   Someone has received an explicit instruction from the Lord.

ii. Someone is making a major doctrinal deviation.

iii. Someone is making a major moral deviation.

It is important to leave a ministry that is suffering from a major doctrinal or moral decay. The Bible says, "a little leaven, leaveneth the whole lump". This means that you will eventually be affected by the presence of evil.

If you have to resign, there are again certain standards of behaviour expected of you.

1. Give ample notice of your intentions to leave the ministry or church.

Your resignation must not be a surprise move. If it comes as a surprise, it is usually an evil and calculated deed.

2. If you must resign, resign alone.

Do not try to influence other people to leave with you. Do not try to win the hearts of people long before you leave, by making special friends all around.

(Defecting pastors love to develop close relationships with vital church members before they leave.) In the end, they leave behind a *confused* group of members who are uncertain about whether to stay or not. They also leave behind a congregation who have to *choose* between their relationship with the departee or their commitment to the church. This is why departing ministers must declare their intentions of resignation long beforehand.

3. Be grateful to the church which you are leaving.

Do not spread bad stories about them after you leave.

Whoso rewardeth evil for good, evil shall not depart from his house.

Proverbs 17:13

4. Do not "muddy" the waters as you leave.

After you have drank from the fresh waters, do not leave behind a pool of contaminated water.

It cannot possibly be that the church, which trained you, and blessed you for many years has suddenly become an evil group. By saying evil things about the church you just left, you 'muddy' the waters and prevent others from being blessed.

Many will no longer receive from the ministry that has blessed you. They will listen to the bad stories you have told and become confused! They will wonder whether your former church has the Holy Spirit or an evil spirit. This is because you have muddied the waters.

No one wants to drink the muddy water. This will invite a curse into your life. The reason why most ministers disappear into oblivion after departure from a major ministry is because they bring upon themselves a curse by the manner in which they leave.

Seemeth it a small thing unto you to have eaten up the good pasture, but ye must tread down with your feet the residue of your pastures? and to have drunk of the deep waters, but ye must foul the residue with your feet?

Ezekiel 34:18

5. Do not start your own ministry in the wrong way.

If you intend to set up a church, you must declare your intentions to the Senior Minister.

However, you must discourage others from following you. Do not set up a church anywhere within a ten-mile radius from where you used to be. It is improper, cheap and unethical to establish a church virtually next door to your mother church. It also smacks of the logic of the jungle to use the same or very similar names that are unique to the church or ministry you are leaving.

The new name should in no way give unclear signals of your recent defection. It must not confuse the members as to where they belong. For instance, if the church you are resigning from is called *Angels Harvest and Healing Center International*, do not call your new church *Angelic Harvesters and Healing Ministry International*.

6. Avoid being cursed when you leave.

Many people cannot rise in the ministry because they are cursed. Many people were cursed the day they left in the wrong way. If you read the bible carefully, you will grow to fear curses. You will also grow to respect the power of a blessing.

Notice that Jacob resigned from Laban's ministry in the wrong way. He left unexpectedly. He left in the wrong way. He left with somebody's children and flocks. Jacob was in great danger of being cursed because of this mistake. Jacob's absence was only detected three days after he left. Jacob almost received a curse for this. God stopped Laban from cursing Jacob just in the nick of time. If God had not intervened, Jacob, the blessed patriarch would have received a curse and Israel would not have become what he became. Many departing pastors earn themselves a solid curse because of the way they go about things. That curse prevents them from ever flourishing, growing or prospering.

And Jacob stole away UNAWARES to Laban the Syrian, in that HE TOLD HIM NOT that he fled. So he fled with all that he had; and he rose up, and passed over the river, and set his face toward the mount Gilead. And it was told Laban on the third day that Jacob was fled.

Genesis 31:20-22

But for God's intervention, Laban could have spoken a curse on Jacob.

IT IS IN THE POWER OF MY HAND TO DO YOU HURT: but the God of your father spake unto me yester-night, saying, Take thou heed that thou speak not to Jacob either good or bad.

Genesis 31:29

Observe that Moses on the other hand, left Jethro's ministry in the right way. He had been in the ministry with him for forty years. Notice also that when it mattered, many years later, Moses could go to Jethro and relate with him normally.

Are you able to go back to the church you left? Do you have a good relationship with the pastor? Does he like you or is he angry with you? Is he happy with you or is he ready to curse you because of how you left him some years ago? Did your departure break the heart of your spiritual father? Did your departure destroy the ministry you left? Have they recovered from your departure? Did you repay good with evil? Did you harm the church you left? Perhaps a curse was never spoken over you but you activated ancient curses that come on people who repay good with evil.

And Moses went and returned to Jethro his father in law, and said unto him, Let me go, I pray thee, and return unto my brethren which are in Egypt, and see whether they be yet alive. And Jethro said to Moses, Go in peace.

Exodus 4:18

Many years later...

And Moses went out to meet his father in law... and they asked each other of their welfare; and they came into the tent... And it came to pass on the morrow, that Moses sat to judge the people: and the people stood by Moses from the morning unto the evening. Hearken now unto my voice [Jethro], I will give thee counsel, and God shall be with thee...

Exodus 18:7, 13, 19

May God establish you in ministry! May you last in ministry!

May you escape the arrows and spears of the enemy!

May you receive your full reward from the Lord Jesus Christ!

CHAPTER 5

Ethics for the Church Service

How is it then, brethren? When ye come together...
Let all things be done unto edifying.

1 Corinthians 14:26

How must we behave when we come together? When not ministering yourself, practice certain basic standards of behaviour. If not, you may intimidate the preacher by your uninvolved attitude. You must therefore consciously and visibly avoid giving an impression of being uninvolved. You might fall into the category of a "know-it-all" person.

1.   **Arrive on time for the church service or meeting.**

Be dressed formally and appropriately for the occasion. Otherwise, the pastor ministering may think that you do not regard his ministration as important. As a visiting minister, you must arrive on time to get a "feel and flow" of the meeting. This will help you to know how to minister. Listening to the choir will also tell you a lot about the church.

2.   **Participate in the worship and do not be a spectator.**

Whenever appropriate, lift up your hands, clap or give a shout of approval.

3.   **Receive the message eagerly.**

Visibly show interest and approval of all that is happening.

4.   **Come to church with your Bible.**

It is important to turn to the passage that is being referred to -- even if you know it already.

5.   **Take notes throughout the sermon even if you know the subject already.**

6.   **Say "Amen" and give other encouraging remarks during the sermon whenever appropriate.**

7.   **Do not yawn, go to sleep or bow down your head during the sermon.**

Do not close your eyes whilst listening to the sermon.

8.   **Unless it is absolutely important, do not get up and leave the service during the sermon only to come back after everything is over.**

9. Do not have a "know-it-all" expression on your face.

During the preaching, smile and laugh whenever appropriate. Do not remain aloof. Do not show that you are above all that is going on.

Notice in the following Scriptures how the looks on a face can interfere with the ministry of an anointed prophet. when you are ministering, it is important to honour certain standards expected of the minister.

BE NOT AFRAID OF THEIR FACES: for I am with thee to deliver thee, saith the LORD.

Jeremiah 1:8

...but they have refused to receive correction: THEY HAVE MADE THEIR FACES HARDER THAN A ROCK...

Jeremiah 5:3

10. You must keep to the purpose for which the meeting is being held.

If it is a worship and teaching service, do not try to introduce deliverance and healing.

11. You must keep to the time stipulated for the service.

If it is a two-hour service, stick to two hours. However, if it is intended to be a long service, do not minister for 30 minutes and then leave. This would be an anti-climax and disappointment to the congregation.

12. Do not push people down.
Should the Lord lead you during the service to pray for individuals in the congregation, do not push people down whilst ministering to them through the laying on of hands.

CHAPTER 6

Ethics for Interacting with Church Members

For I determined not to know any thing among you, save Jesus Christ, and him crucified.

1 Corinthians 2:2

The pastor must always be aware of the fact that he is a *shepherd*, and church members are sheep. There are many respects in which the sheep cannot and must not relate to the shepherd. This is because they are essentially different. A shepherd can best relate to other shepherds in certain social and private matters.

The shepherd's interaction with the sheep must be limited to his professional role as a shepherd to the sheep. As such, the minister must restrict his interactions with church members to that which concerns the salvation of their souls and their establishment in Christ. Resolve to "know nothing" among your people save Jesus Christ and Him crucified (1 Corinthians 2:2).

Observe the following standards therefore in your relationships with church members:

1. **Don't visit people because you are hungry.**

   Your visit to church members' houses should relate to the salvation of their souls. Do not roam from house to house in order to wine and dine.

2. **Respect your church members' privacy.**

   You should also respect your church members' privacy, and not venture into certain areas of their homes unless specifically invited to.

   In certain cases, you may be invited into a bedroom to pray for a sick person. If you invade your church members' privacy, they will also invade your privacy.

   If you go into their kitchens and bedrooms, they will also expect to come to yours. When they do, you will not be able to control them.

3. **Be careful when paying impromptu visits.**

   A surprise visit may catch someone unprepared. The home may be in disarray and the people may be inappropriately dressed. In such a case, excuse yourself immediately to allow them to get ready. Do not embarrass your church members.

...and he (Noah) was uncovered within his tent. ...Shem and Japheth... ...WENT BACKWARD... and they saw not their father's nakedness.

Genesis 9:21, 23

4. **Do not give the impression that you like a lot of food.**

   Do not give the impression that you are hungry, or that you would be happy if they would serve you some of their nice things.

5. **Do not honour invitations to dinner on a completely empty stomach.**

   You may have to eat at home before the dinner so that you will not look like a hungry lion. Do not give the impression that all pastors are hungry and poverty-stricken. Although your host may encourage you to eat as much as you can, they will think, "What a greedy man this is!" when you eat too much.

   ...Eat and drink, saith he to thee; but his heart is not with thee.

   Proverbs 23:7

6. **Do not lick your plate.** If you are in a situation where you are obliged to eat, do not lick your plate clean. Do not chew all the bones, as you probably would at home.

   When thou sittest to eat with a ruler, consider diligently what is before thee: And put a knife to thy throat, if thou be a man given to appetite. Be not desirous of his dainties...

   Proverbs 23:1-3

7. **Do not ask for additional food once you have finished eating.**

Again, they will readily serve you but will think to themselves, "This Pastor is greedy!"

8. There are times you should avoid eating in public.

Perhaps just nibbling at something may be appropriate.

9. Do not insult or abuse a church member.

Do not shout at your church members or quarrel with them. Avoid gaining the reputation of a cantankerous person.

For a bishop must be blameless... not soon angry... no striker...

Titus 1:7

10. Do not strike or slap your church members.

You must never fight physically with your members even if they are insolent. Learn to commend people to God and to time.

Not a hard drinker nor given to BLOWS.
1 Timothy 3:3 (Weymouth Translation)

11. Be very careful when settling disputes between church members.

There is a tendency for one of them to think that you are siding with the other against him/her.

12. Do not become a debt collector on behalf of a church member.

Things may turn nasty, and you may find yourself right in the middle of a squabble between members of your congregation!

...neither be partaker of other men's sins: keep thyself pure.
1 Timothy 5:22

13. Be careful when settling disputes between husbands and wives.

Marital conflicts are like the flu. They come and go by themselves. Often, the couple will settle their disputes anyway, without much interference. In other words, do not take sides or even appear to take sides.

Do not say bad things about one partner to the other. Later, they may jointly perceive you as an enemy of their marriage.

CHAPTER 7

Ethics for Relating with the Opposite Sex

Rebuke not an elder, but intreat him as a father; and the younger men as brethren; The elder women as mothers; the younger as sisters, with all purity

1 Timothy 5:1-2

Relationships with the opposite sex have always been a problem area for ministers. It is important that all ministers honour the standards of behaviour outlined in the Word of God concerning opposite sex relations. Common sense also teaches us how to relate with the opposite sex. Samson had unethical interactions with the opposite sex; this eventually led to the demise of his ministry.

Observe therefore the following standards in your relationships with the opposite sex:

1. **As far as possible, do not minister to the opposite sex when you are alone.**

   Have somebody with you all the time! Remember that Jesus sent out His disciples in pairs. This will protect you from accusations and possible temptations.

   All things are lawful for me, but all things are not expedient...
   1 Corinthians 10:23

2. **As much as possible, do not counsel the opposite sex alone and behind closed doors.**

   Leave the doors to your office open if you are alone with the opposite sex. Again, this is for your own protection.

   Abstain from all appearance of evil.
   1 Thessalonians 5:22

3. **Do not have a habit or pattern of giving strange women rides alone in your car.** Do not habitually pick up young ladies from the roadside and offer them rides. This could lead to an extra-marital affair.

4. **Do not discuss your personal life and marital problems with church members of the opposite sex.**

   This will only lead to intimate relationships with people who should not be close to you.

5. **Do not have the habit of going on social outings alone with a member of the opposite sex who is not your spouse.**

   It will only raise questions about whether you are having an improper relationship with that person.

6. **If you are a male minister, do not minister to a lady by laying hands on her private parts.**

   Can a man take fire in his bosom, and his clothes not be burned?

   Proverbs 6:27

CHAPTER 8

Ethics for Relating with External Ministers

And the eye cannot say unto the hand, I have no need
of thee...

1 Corinthians 12:21

I n the ministry, it is necessary to relate with other ministers who may not be in your church or denomination. God wants to expose you to other ministry gifts. As much as possible, try to have a good relationship with all ministers. Often, isolation occurs because one has been hurt in the early stages of ministry. Many ministers run into a corner and hide in order to escape being despised.

Isolation can work together for your good in the ministry for the following reasons:

i.   You will be able to concentrate on your ministry.

ii.   You will avoid being despised, disregarded and discouraged all the time by other so-called successful ministers.

iii. You will be able to avoid the distractions of inter-church politics.

iv.   You will be able to avoid the wholesale adoption of o t h e r ministers' mistakes.

v.   You will be able to develop your unique identity and calling.

vi.   You will be able to avoid being submerged under the banners of other domineering pastors who are trying to gain supremacy and lordship over God's heritage in the city.

vii. Isolation will force you to learn biblical rather than human standards for all aspects of life and ministry.

Isolation can also work against you in the ministry for the following reasons:

i.   You will need the input, ideas and the gifts of other ministers.

ii.   You may be able to learn a great deal from other successful pastors in your city. I have learnt a lot from those directly ahead of me in my city. I have watched and learnt from their mistakes and successes. I do things in my church that I have learnt from other ministers.

... that they without us should not be made perfect.
                                                    Hebrews 11:40

Because of all these, you have to develop delicate but important relationships with external ministers. For these important relationships to exist, every minister must adopt an important set of standards.

Observe the following standards in your relationships with external ministers:

1. **Do not speak evil of any minister or church, especially from the pulpit or in public.** If you have anything to say about a church or denomination, say something positive.

   ...speak evil of no man...
                                                    Titus 3:2

2. **If you are led to speak against an unscriptural practice of a church or ministry, try not to mention the name of that church.** Expose wrong practices with balanced biblical truths.

3. **Do not criticize or ridicule other ministers in front of the congregation.**

   Remember that as you do so, you also set the stage for others to criticize you in the future. Even when David had the opportunity to kill Saul, he did not. He demonstrated to his followers that kings must not be killed --even if they are wrong. Later, when David made the mistake of murdering Uriah, the other mighty men did not rise up and kill David, because they had learnt by example not to kill the king. David had taught them an important principle: do not lift up your sword, finger or tongue against God's anointed servants.

   ...Touch not mine anointed, and do my prophets no harm.
                                                    1 Chronicles 16:22

4. **Expose your church to other ministry gifts.** Do not let the feeling of insecurity overwhelm you. As you open up your church to other gifts, the church will be blessed and grow larger.

   ...the whole body fitly joined together and compacted by that which every joint supplieth... MAKETH INCREASE of the body...

   Ephesians 4:16

5. **If you are not absolutely certain of a minister in terms of what he will say or do, then you might as well not invite him to your church.** Do not invite ministers who want to use your church as a launching pad to start a church near you – Do not invite ministers who want to steal some of your members!

6. **Give honour and respect to all external ministers.** One very good way of showing respect to a minister is to invite him honourably.

   ...honour to whom honour.

   Romans 13:7

7. **Learn the features of an *honourable* invitation.**

i. Invite the minister to an important and well-attended service or function.

   Do not invite someone you want to honour to a minor function. For example, a youth service, or the morning session of a convention.

ii. Unless impossible, be present at the service for which you invited the person.

   Try not to invite a minister if you know you will be absent (especially when building a new relationship).

iii. The Senior Pastor should introduce the visiting minister himself.

iv.   During the introduction, refer to your guest by his official title, i.e., the title he has accorded himself.

Do not refer to him as Reverend Agegebodavari when he refers to himself as Chief Apostle Agegebodavari.

v.   Find out his full name and pronounce it properly.

vi.   Use the full and proper name of his church and ministry.

For instance, do not say he is the Pastor of *The Light Church* when he is the Pastor of *Lighthouse Chapel International*. There is a big difference between the two!

8.   **Do not be surprised if you are unable to establish relationships with some ministers.** Ministerial relationships are just like the relationships between friends. Some people can be your friends, and others simply will not flow with you. Do not be surprised if some ministers shun you in spite of your success.

This could be because you intimidate them. They may be afraid of you. This is natural, and they express it by shunning you.

9.   **Show respect to any pastor who visits your church, even if he is not a speaker.**

Ministers of the gospel are very insecure. It is important to acknowledge their presence in the service. You can do this by:

i.   Asking them to stand and wave to the church.

ii.   Inviting them on stage to say "hello" to the church.

10. **Show respect to all seniors in the ministry.** You can do this by:

i.   Acknowledging their presence in the service.

ii.   Inviting them to minister, if the occasion permits.

iii. Do not call a senior forward to lay hands on him or to pray for him.

...the less is blessed of the better.

Hebrews 7:7

iv.   Do not refer to a senior by an old nickname.

v.   Refer to him by his title and not by his first name.

11. Avoid inter-church politics.

There is a lot of political rivalry between pastors in cities. This destructive but real phenomenon is prevalent in the Church today. It is something that all ministers must be aware of and keep themselves from.

You will notice the lobbying for pre-eminence and lordship over God's heritage by some ministers. You must not let the desire for power dictate your relationship with other ministers. That will hinder the development of real friendships.

...Diotrephes...loveth to have the preeminence among them...

3 John 9

Avoid joining rival ministerial camps. These camps are cliques of minister friends who get on well with each other. Those who do not "fit in" are not accorded a certain level of respect and recognition. It is important to have good relationships with many ministers without joining their political camps.

12. Show respect to junior colleagues in the ministry. Not every junior minister is your son in the ministry. Even if the junior minister is your son in the Lord, it is not always appropriate to refer to him as your son or daughter.

i.   Refer to them in public by their titles.

ii.   Do not refer to everybody as your son in the ministry.

iii. Never correct or rebuke a junior minister in public.

iv. Correct them in private, out of the view of the congregation. If you correct them in public you will undermine their authority and confidence.

v. Praise your junior ministers in public, this will bring out the best in them.

Render therefore TO ALL their dues... honour to whom honour.
Romans 13:7

CHAPTER 9

Ethics for Handling Visiting Ministers

And as ye would that men should do to you, do ye also to them likewise.

Luke 6:31

T he visiting minister is a very important person and must be treated as such. Unfortunately, many resident pastors do not know how to relate appropriately to visiting ministers. This is often because they have never been visiting preachers themselves. The wrong handling of a visiting minister often leads to offences and the destruction of already fragile ministerial relationships.

1. **Invite ministers personally and follow it up with a letter.** Some people are offended when you do not write to them or speak to them personally. For some people, the one without the other is not enough.

2. **The visiting minister should be welcomed at his point of entry.** If the external minister is coming from another location, as much as possible a minister of his rank must receive him at the airport, station, etc. For example, if he is a head pastor, then the senior minister of the inviting church must meet him. This also applies when the minister is departing. When the minister arrives in church, a minister of corresponding rank must welcome him. If this is not possible, an important delegation must do so.

3. **The visiting minister should sit next to the inviting minister.**

4. **Refer to the invited minister by the official designation he has accorded himself.** If his title is General Overseer, do not refer to him as the General Superintendent. If he refers to himself as an Apostle, do not call him a Pastor.

5. **Know the full name of your invited guest.** You must pronounce it correctly.

6. **Identify and introduce the visiting minister's delegation.** It is important to acknowledge them as well. Do not disregard people's associates. You may be disregarding a future Elisha.

7. **The visiting minister's wife should be welcomed nicely.** She is an important person.

8. **Use the proper name of the invited minister's church.** Not remembering the correct name gives the impression that you are dealing with an unimportant church with an unfortunately laborious name that you cannot bother to remember.

9. **Give the external minister adequate time to minister.** For example, do not give a guest minister 10 minutes to minister, when he has travelled ten thousand kilometres to minister in your church.

10. **Introduce your guest minister with excitement.**

    Let the church welcome the visitor with great expectation in their hearts.

11. **Outline and explain specifically to the external minister any function or expectation you may have of him.** For example, if you want him to raise funds, make altar calls, ordain pastors, etc., discuss this with him in detail before he arrives. Do not surprise your guest. Some people are so melancholic that they need to know everything months in advance.

12. **All conditions of the external minister's visit should be clearly defined prior to his arrival/acceptance to minister.** This includes financial, transportation, and accommodation arrangements. The minister must be given the option to decide whether he will come in spite of the conditions that you are offering him.

13. **The honorarium and all expenses can and must be discussed in many cases before the minister accepts the invitation.** This is especially important if the minister is travelling a long distance. You may wrongly assume that the visiting minister will only incur the cost of his plane ticket.

    But you may not know that he had to, for example, travel in a rented car 300-km to the airport and sleep in a hotel overnight in order to catch the plane in the morning. All of these are hidden expenses, which must be discussed.

It is very sad for a minister to travel several miles, minister from his heart, only to return with new unexpected debts.

Even so hath the Lord ordained that they which preach the gospel should live of the gospel.

1 Corinthians 9:14

A good honorarium should include expenses and blessings. The honorarium must bless and encourage the minister financially. A visiting minister's rank also determines what a good honorarium is. If the person is a very senior minister, the honorarium must be correspondingly substantial.

A good honorarium is calculated by the number of days a person ministers. A good honorarium is also determined by the impact of the visiting minister's ministry. Honorariums should not be given to the visiting minister in full public view. The minister should be given the honorarium in private and by the appropriate person. The visiting minister may sign a voucher or receipt for the honorarium (for accounting purposes).

The honorarium should be prepared before the meeting. This is to avoid very long delays in paying the honorarium. Some churches even forget to pay any honorarium at all. It is often more difficult to pay the honorarium long after the minister has left than it is to pay immediately after the programme. It is decent to present an accompanying thank you letter with the honorarium.

14. **The visiting minister should be refreshed briefly and then politely escorted away.**

CHAPTER 10

Ethics for the Travelling Minister

Whensoever I take my journey into Spain, I will
come to you: for I trust to see you in my journey,
and to be brought on my way thitherward by you,
if first I be somewhat filled with your company.
Romans 15:24

Apostle Paul was a travelling minister journeying up and down for the gospel. Many people are called into the travelling ministry today. It is important to learn how to be a good travelling minister. When you are a travelling minister, you must conduct yourself in an ethical fashion. Be conscious of the fact that you are God's ambassador.

You must work closely with the host pastor. Do not be surprised if he is inexperienced in relating with, and handling travelling ministers. He may not have had the experience of being a travelling minister himself.

Maintain therefore the following ethical standards when you are a travelling minister:

1. **Show respect to ministers and churches to which you have been invited:**

   When called to speak, find something nice to say about the host's church, the pastor and the choir.

   Praise them for all of their efforts. Do not say things that make the host's church look inferior. For example, do not say, "Our youth choir is larger than this entire church!"

   Do not call the host pastor to pray for him, unless the relationship or the spiritual order so dictates (e.g. if you are a father to the person in the ministry). He may have a smaller church than you do but he may not see you as a father or someone who has the spiritual authority to lay hands on him.

2. **Do not invite yourself to minister in other people's churches.**

   Avoid being pushy and forward, claiming that you want to be a blessing to them. Always wait for the 'door' to be opened, or the invitation to be given. Even after the 'door' is opened, ensure that you minister where the Spirit of the Lord directs you.

3. **Never allow the lure of generous honorariums to become your primary reason for ministering.**

Do not demand money. Jesus said, "Freely ye have received, freely give" (Matt. 10:8b). Do not demand a certain sum of money as a precondition for you to minister! Although this is a common practice, be honest with yourself - it gives the impression that you are a commercial motivational speaker.

4. **Do not misuse the exposure given you by this invitation.**

Whoso rewardeth evil for good, evil shall not depart from his house.

Proverbs 17:13

To have a hidden agenda of starting a church or ministry nearby with some of your host pastor's members is tantamount to striking your friend below the belt. The travelling minister must be grateful for the visibility and exposure granted him by all invitations. You must not repay the good done to you with evil. Do not take an offering for yourself. Many people will be offended when you raise partners or raise an offering for your ministry in their church. You can only do such a thing if you have been given the permission to do so.

5. **In a diplomatic and polite manner, ensure that you will not be mistreated.**

Because many pastors do not travel themselves, they often don't take into account the real costs that travelling ministers incur. It is good to clarify the conditions in an undemanding way before making a final commitment to participate in the programme. This is especially important when you do not have a long-standing relationship with the minister in question. Sometimes you cannot be sure of how you will be treated. However, if you already have a cordial relationship with the inviting minister, these clarifications are not necessary.

6. **Do not promote yourself. Show appreciation to the host pastor and to the church in which you are ministering.**

Remember that the pastor must have put in a lot of work to develop a congregation capable of hosting a travelling minister. The host pastor will have promoted and advertised you in a favourable way. You will most likely have a good reception as a visiting minister. People receive visiting ministers with more faith and expectation. In your presentation, do not try to outshine or make the host pastor look inferior.

...a prophet hath no honour in his own country.
John 4:44

7. **Flow with the theme of the programme to which you have been invited.**

You must do this unless the host pastor specifically gives you a freehand to minister on anything you want to. Flow with the specific purpose of the services.

There are teaching services, evangelistic meetings, anointing services, as well as miracle and healing services. These are all different types of meetings. For example, do not try to have a miracle service when a teaching seminar has been planned.

If you have been asked just to make an altar call, do not hold an anointing service. This would be totally out of place, and will not be well received. Let your host clarify exactly what he expects of you in the service.

You may be asked to perform a specific function such as fund-raising. If you have been asked to raise funds, do not give a sermon in addition to that. Someone else may preach the sermon.

8. **Find out any cultural differences you may have to respect in the city you are visiting.**

For instance, in certain cities it is not safe to conduct services late into the night because of crime in the city. In other places, services can continue late into the night without any danger to the congregation.

9. **Promote and lift up the ministry of your host. Do not just use the pulpit to promote your own ministry. Remember that real promotion comes from the Lord and not from man.**

   For promotion cometh neither from the east, nor from the west, nor from the south.

   Psalm 75:6

   At the end of the programme, the church you are visiting should be edified and encouraged. They must not feel despised or condemned. Your ministry should result in the church being uplifted and motivated. You can judge your ethical performance in a very simple way - if the host pastor invites you back!

10. **Invite people who invite you.**

    You must plan to give a corresponding invitation to the one who invites you. Do not think you are the only one who has something to offer!

CHAPTER 11

Financial Ethics

For the love of money is the root of all evil: which
while some coveted after, they have erred from the
faith, and pierced themselves through with many
sorrows.

1 Timothy 6:10

Many criticisms levelled against us because of finances. We cannot avoid criticism but we must minimize the opportunities that people have to speak against us. We therefore, need to adopt certain standards and ethics in the area of finances. So that ye may be blameless and harmless, the sons of God, without rebuke, in the midst of a crooked and perverse nation, among whom ye shine as lights in the world; (Philippians 2:15).

1. **Pay your tithes and give offerings generously as a good pastor.**

   You are a hypocrite if you do not pay tithes and offerings yourself (teaching one thing, and doing another). This may sound obvious, but many pastors do not pay their tithes.

2. **Do not receive money on behalf of the church.**

   Ask the church members to put their tithes and offerings directly into the offering basket. Your pocket is not an offering bowl!

3. **Do not personally count the offerings.**

   You will appear greedy and very interested in the money.

4. **Do not allow money to be counted in the full view of everyone in church.**

   Some people may think the church has a lot of money, or others may be tempted to steal from the church.

5. **Do not take Sunday's, or any other offering to your house.**

   It will seem as though all the offerings are being given to you personally. If the money were stolen from your home, you would have created for yourself a neat little scandal. There would be little anyone could say in your defence.

6. **If you receive an unusually large gift, personally or in the offering (for instance, an expensive car) you must question the source of it.**

The money could be from a dubious source. Receiving it could lead you into some serious problems.

7. Generally speaking, do not borrow money. Try to manage with what you have.

Do not borrow money from the church nor from the offerings. You may be accused of stealing from the church.

8. Do not borrow money from church members.

Do not borrow cars, televisions, or other material items from church members. Church members will lend things to you with a smile, but they may lose their respect for you.

The rich ruleth over the poor, and the borrower is servant to the lender.

Proverbs 22:7

9. Do not ask church members for material things or for money.

This is also offensive. E.g., "Can I have one of your radios since you have two and I don't have one?

10. Do not receive money on behalf of church members.

Do not hold church members' money for safekeeping. You are not a bank. What will you say if the money gets lost?

11. Do not act as a surety or guarantor for your church members.

Do not bail someone just because he is your church member. This is very risky as all sorts of people find their way into churches. You may find yourself in prison for trying to help your church member (who may be a bona fide criminal).

He that is surety for a stranger shall smart for it: and he that hateth suretiship is sure.

Proverbs 11:15

12. Do not lend money to church members.

If a church member asks you for money, give what you can without expecting any repayment. What you give may be a percentage of the original sum requested. This is better than lending money because when it is time to reclaim it, you may find all kinds of ugly situations developing. You may even lose your church member in the process of getting your money back!

13. Do not allow money and gifts to be the basis of relationships you have with people.

Such relationships are very unstable. Therefore, do not give unusually special treatment to rich people.

14. Do not demand or charge a fee as a condition for praying for someone or for prophesying to him.

... freely ye have received, freely give.

Matthew 10:8

Find a decent and honourable way of receiving free-will offerings to ensure that your motives are not misjudged.

15. Do not ask people directly how much they earn or how much they have.

This could be offensive.

16. Do not announce your salary and assets publicly.

Revealing your possessions may be dangerous in a culture of jealousy and poverty. People may not understand why you should have what you have, especially if they don't have some of the things you have.

And Hezekiah...SHEWED THEM ALL THE HOUSE OF HIS PRECIOUS THINGS...and all that was found in his treasures: there was nothing in his house, nor in all his dominion, that Hezekiah shewed them not.

Then came Isaiah ... and said unto him... Behold, the days come, that all that is in thine house... shall be carried into Babylon: nothing shall be left, saith the LORD.

2 Kings 20:13, 14, 17

17. Your financial needs should not affect your preaching and speech.

Your preaching should not include insinuations about your lack of money. Some pastors do this in order to gain sympathy and receive donations.

Even so hath the Lord ordained that they which preach the gospel should live of the gospel. But I have used none of these things: NEITHER HAVE I WRITTEN THESE THINGS, THAT IT SHOULD BE SO DONE UNTO ME...

1 Corinthians 9:14, 15

18. If you make a large financial pledge do not announce it publicly.

Again, people may not understand, how come you have so much money. You may not have the opportunity to explain the source of all your blessings.

CHAPTER 12

Ethics for Receiving of Gifts

But I have all, and abound:I am full, having received of Epaphroditus the things which were sent from you, an odour of a sweet smell, a sacrifice acceptable, wellpleasing to God.

Philippians 4:18

The pastor stands as a minister representing God. It is common for pastors to receive offerings and gifts. The bible teaches Christians to honour their pastors who teach them the word of God. "Let him that is taught in the word communicate unto him that teacheth in all good things." (Galatians 6:6).

The pastor must therefore, honour and respect certain standards of behaviour in regards to receiving of gifts.

1. **Acknowledge all gifts that you receive.** If you do not, the church members will think that the gift meant nothing to you.

   They may also think that you did not receive the gift at all. If the gift comes from the church, you must thank the whole church. Notice how Paul acknowledged the gift he received from the Philippians.

   But I have all, and abound: I am full, having received of Epaphroditus the things which were sent from you, an odour of a sweet smell, a sacrifice acceptable, well-pleasing to God.

   Philippians 4:18

2. **Do not give the impression that you do not appreciate gifts.**

   It is biblical for people to honour you with their substance after you have ministered the word of God to them. If you receive a gift that you do not particularly need or like don't give the impression that you do not appreciate it. Say, "thank you" and be appreciative. Do not give people the impression that you are ungrateful or proud.

3. **Beware of unusual gifts.** Some criminals may want to dispose of ill-gotten gain by passing it on to the pastor or the church. You may get into trouble with the authorities if you accept certain gifts.

CHAPTER 13

The Ethics of Privacy

And Hezekiah hearkened unto them, and SHEWED THEM ALL THE HOUSE OF HIS PRECIOUS THINGS, the silver, and the gold, and the spices, and the precious ointment, and all the house of his armour, and all that was found in his treasures:there was nothing in his house, nor in all his dominion, that Hezekiah shewed them not.

Then came Isaiah the prophet unto king Hezekiah, and said unto him, What said these men? and from whence came they unto thee? And Hezekiah said, They are come from a far country, even from Babylon.

And he said, WHAT HAVE THEY SEEN IN THINE HOUSE? And Hezekiah answered, All the things that are in mine house have they seen:there is nothing among my treasures that I have not shewed them. And Isaiah said unto Hezekiah, Hear the word of the Lord. Behold, the days come, that all that is in thine house, and that which thy fathers have laid up in store unto this day, shall be carried into Babylon:nothing shall be left, saith the Lord

2 Kings 20:13-17

Privacy is very important in the ministry. Hezekiah showed everything he had to the enemy and paid a high price for that. Attention must be given to maintain and protect your privacy from being violated by anyone. This principle includes privacy from church members. Your house is your castle and should be your bastion of safety and privacy.

Observe therefore the following standards in relation to maintaining your privacy:

1. Do not allow just anyone to visit you in your home.

Restrict the stream of visitors to your home. Any minister who has lots of people coming to his home will discover that he is exposing himself to dangerous attacks. It is common for church members to discuss what they did and saw in their pastor's house.

2. Do not turn your home into a church office.

Official church business must be done at the office of the church. Do not turn your home into another church office! Those allowed to visit you at home must not be given access to any area of the house that you consider exclusive. Maintaining your privacy will help maintain your self-respect.

Privacy will protect you from many of the long-standing enemies of ministers.

These include: the media, bitter critics, jealous friends, carnal church members and envious colleague pastors. You will also be shielded from constant analysis of your material possessions by outsiders.

Notice what happened to Eglon the King of Moab when he allowed people to come into his private apartment- he lost his life!

And Ehud came unto him (Eglon, the king of Moab); and he was sitting in a SUMMER PARLOUR, WHICH HE HAD FOR HIMSELF ALONE… And Ehud put forth his left hand, and took the dagger from his right thigh, and thrust it into his belly.

Judges 3:20-21

CHAPTER 14

Ethics for Public Appearance

…that ye may have somewhat to answer them which glory in appearance, and not in heart.

2 Corinthians 5:12

In this secular world, you will be assessed by your physical appearance --whether you like it or not. No one can see into the spirit realm. Even Christians do not see your spiritual depth. God looks on the heart. Man looks on the outside. As for man, he has always looked on the outside, and will continue to look on the outside. Do not let your external appearance drive people away from Christ, or dissuade others from becoming ministers.

1. **Develop the art of dressing decently and formally, even when casual.** Thus, you will never be out of place when called on for official duty without notice.

   ...be instant in season, out of season...
   2 Timothy 4:2

2. **Do not appear extravagant or ostentatious.** The hallmark of greatness is simplicity.

3. **When preaching on Sundays, you should be properly dressed.**

   ...the priest, whom he shall anoint... SHALL PUT ON THE LINEN CLOTHES, even the holy garments.
   Leviticus 16:32

4. **Own a decent car.** Acquire a safe car; your life is precious. If the shepherd goes, the sheep will scatter--and the devil knows it. People will criticize you even if you sit on a donkey.

   There is an evil which I have seen under the sun, as an error which proceedeth from the ruler: Folly is set in great dignity, and the rich sit in low place. I have seen servants upon horses, and princes walking as servants upon the earth.
   Ecclesiastes 10:5-7

5. **Acquire an appropriate car.** Do not be afraid to treat yourself with respect. It is your own mistake if you fail to treat yourself with respect.

Whatever you do, people will criticize you, so do not be deterred by the fear of criticism. Please meditate on these verses and the Lord will give you understanding.

6. **Do not use the most expensive car in the city.** Neither should it be the most fantastic, expensive or luxurious of all the cars in the city. If this happens, you may have problems with the usual enemies of the Church.

7. **Do not drive other people's cars.** As much as possible, do not drive another person's car. If you damage someone else's car, you may be unable to repair it. If you do not have a car, manage until you get one.

8. **Do not acquire a car you cannot afford.** Do not live above your income. Cut your coat according to your size!

That ye may approve things that are excellent; that ye may be sincere and without offence till the day of Christ;

Philippians 1:10

CHAPTER 15

Ethics for Handling
Outsiders

**Walk in wisdom toward them that are without,
redeeming the time. Let your speech be alway with
grace, seasoned with salt, that ye may know how ye
ought to answer every man**

Colossians 4:5-6

As a church grows and becomes more influential, even the government will take an interest in the church. There may even be spies sent to monitor what is going on in the church. Our religion has a way of making us political. This is because we have to speak against injustice and corruption. Be wise, and realize that you are a political force to reckon with. Rise up and fulfil your calling. You are called to influence people!

1. **Pray for the king.**

   It is our God-given duty to pray for the 'king' or leader of the nation. The Bible teaches us to pray for those who are in authority (not those who are seeking to come into the place of authority!).

   I exhort therefore, that, first of all, supplications, prayers, intercessions, and giving of thanks be made for all men; for kings...

   1 Timothy 2:1, 2

2. **Do not tell your church members whom to vote for.**

   Preach the truth and leave them to decide for themselves.

3. **Do not attend political rallies, even if you support their party.**

   Do not display political paraphernalia. By wearing political party uniforms, you make yourself into a political activist rather than a preacher of the Gospel.

4. **Traditionally you should remain neutral. But there are times, when it may be necessary to openly declare your stand.**

   This must be done in a way that does not resemble a political campaign. Avoid becoming a political activist. You are a preacher! Stay with your call! [77]Do not allow yourself to be used to divide the body of Christ into political camps.